BEAR

Chrissy Williams is a poet, editor and tutor living in London. She has published a number of pamphlets, including *Flying into the Bear* (Happen*Stance* Press, 2013) which was shortlisted for the Michael Marks Awards, *Epigraphs* (if p then q, 2014) which was featured on BBC Radio 3's *The Verb*, and *ANGELA* (Sidekick Books, 2013) which fuses *Murder, She Wrote* with *Twin Peaks*. Her first book-length collection, *Bear*, was published by Bloodaxe Books in 2017.

She has worked in books, magazines, at the Poetry Library at Southbank Centre, and as a Visiting Lecturer in Creative Writing. She is director of the annual Free Verse: Poetry Book Fair and founded the world's first bespoke edible poetry journal *Poetry Digest*. She also edited the UK's first book on poetry comics, *Over the Line: An Introduction to Poetry Comics* (Sidekick Books, 2015) and currently works as a comics editor.

She is half-Italian and she likes bears.

www.chrissywilliams.blogspot.com
www.twitter.com/chrissywilliams

CHRISSY WILLIAMS

BEAR

BLOODAXE BOOKS

ISBN: 978 1 78037 332 4

First published 2017 by
Bloodaxe Books Ltd,
Eastburn,
South Park,
Hexham,
Northumberland NE46 1BS.

www.bloodaxebooks.com
For further information about Bloodaxe titles
please visit our website or write to
the above address for a catalogue.

Supported using public funding by
ARTS COUNCIL
ENGLAND

Cover artwork by Tom Humberstone, www.tomhumberstone.com

Printed in Great Britain by Bell & Bain Limited, Glasgow, Scotland, on
acid-free paper sourced from mills with FSC chain of custody certification.

CONTENTS

9   Bear of the Artist

10   LOVE

11   Gone

15   Robot Unicorn Attack

16   JON SPENCER BLUES EXPLOSION in the Spring

17   The Lost

18   Green Lake

19   Bliss

21   Sonnet for *Zookeeper*

23   On Getting Boney M's Cover of 'Mary's Boy Child' by Harry Belafonte Stuck in My Head

24   Sheep

25   *from* Groundhog Day

28   The art of editing

29   Poem in Which I Respond to Notes in the Margins of Ian Hamilton Finlay's *Selections*

31   Bedroom Filled With Foam

32   Wet Days Are the Worst

33   Over Dave's Trousers

34   Jam Trap

35   Where Have You Put the Wine?

36   Four Hours Away

37   Digital Ghost Towns

39   Reading Your Comics in Eype

40   The Burning of the Houses

41   Menagerie Speeches

44   Bird Talk

45   Post

47   There Is an Epigraph

48   Moorhens

50   Art Imitates Life, but Life Imitates TV

51   Murder, She Wrote

54   Manifesto Based on Notes from Lars von Trier's
       Five Obstructions

55   Tigers

57   Tin Can Odyssey

58   Go

60   The Invisible Bear

61   Stage Directions for *The Dog Always Wins*

for you
who also live and die
by the bear

For small creatures such as we
the vastness is bearable only through love.

CARL SAGAN, *Contact*

Bear of the Artist

I asked the artist to draw me a heart and instead he drew a bear.

I asked him, 'What kind of heart is this?' and he said, 'It's not a
heart at all.'

I asked him, 'What kind of bear is this?' and he said, 'It's not a
bear either.'

I asked him, 'What kind of artist are you anyway?' and he said,

'I am the one who exists to put bears in your head, who exists

to put ideas in your head in place of bears, who mistrusts anyone

who tells you they know what kind of place the heart is, the head,

how it should look, what size, what stopping distances, etc.,

and as long as you keep me existing to put bears in your head

I will, because nights are getting darker, and we're all tired,

we're all so tired, and everyone could use a bear sometimes,

everyone could use a wild bear, though they can be dangerous

and there's nothing worse than a bear in the face, when it breaks –

always remember how your bear breaks down

against the shore, the shore, the shore.'

LOVE

Where the market stall sells gift wrap
bearing the word LOVE, just LOVE,
I saw somebody I thought was you
and, in a flash, you were gone again,
a thrust to the chest in pinks and reds.
In front, the pigeons pecked at crumbs,
flinging them in arcs across the ground,
the drawn-out moment scored in air.
The floor turned to water, unsteady seas,
the word LOVE, just LOVE, repeating.

Gone

(after Egill Skallagrimsson's 'Sonatorrek')

The tongue is a set of scales weighing up language.

The poet is tongue-tied, blocked in the face of grief.

Words are difficult to draw out from this sorrow.

Yet some words come.

*

word stuck
tongue locked
taste blocked
laugh struck
mead mucked
the light touch
the word
is also
just
a word

*

No man is happy who carries the corpse of his family.

There is a natural order to things where a man buries his parents.

When a child dies before his parents, a hole is made in the world.

The sea has broken a hole in the wall of my family.

*

to fill a hole in the head with oceans
to call shape to the clouds in metal
to raise steel to the seas for carving

to turn days into wind for chasing
to steal mead from giants for telling
to give dogs to the tongue at twilight
to bring bears to the heart by moonlight
to draw bears to the head

*

I must commemorate and share the memory of my son.

My son, who was lost from the world before he became a man,
  was a good son.

I am reminded of loss, of death, in the midst of life's most urgent
  moments.

'It often comes to me in the moon's bear's fair wind.'

*

the moon
the moon the bear
the moon the bear the fair wind
        the moon the bear the fair breath
the moon the bear the fair wind
        the moon the bear the fair breath
the moon
the moon

*

Now I am bad company for all men.

But I am not angry. My son has gone to join my ancestors.

Thoughts of my grief and my grief's expression

weigh heavily on me.

*

I had this bear, you know?
Like, a bear in my head
that I carried round with me
and more bears everywhere, but not the soft kind,
I mean with teeth, so like,
they were all " "
like, a bear with teeth.
Did you ever stare at the moon like it's a face?
Did you ever see a bear moon smile?
I, like, don't know for sure, right,
but I think the moon moves the water?
It, like, raises oceans,
then crushes them all with a single look.
Every night I feel the bear breathing
warm air on my, like, neck or something.
I've never been afraid of bears
and I'm not now.

*

I acknowledge the gift of language which has been given to me.

I acknowledge the skill in language which has been gifted to me,

the language with which I can uncover truth.

*

Now, in facing these difficulties I see death.

I see death standing before me on the hill.

I shall gladly, unconcernedly and with goodwill

wait, smile for her.

Words do not express thoughts very well…
And yet it also pleases me and seems right
that what is of value and wisdom to one man
seems nonsense to another.

HERMANN HESSE, *Siddhartha*

Robot Unicorn Attack

(a love poem for a videogame)

Possibility bursts like a horse
full of light, accelerating
into a star. Explosion. Hit
<X> to make your dreams
crash into stone. Death.
Diatonic chimes of joy.
I want to be with you.
Let dolphins fly in time.
Swim through air, leap
past sense, past sin and then
hit <Z> to chase your dreams
again. *Always. Harmony.* Up,
smash goes the rainbow-trailing
heart again. Again. Again, again!
I want to be with you when
make-believe is possible.
I want to be with you when
robot unicorns never cry, hit
stars collapse in quiet love.
When there is only love.
Harmony. No shame.

JON SPENCER BLUES EXPLOSION
in the Spring

We lean into the soft brake BLUES
as you flip the indicator on
JON at the corner where four roads meet
in front of the old farm. SPENCER
Mountains slouch behind, BLUES
reluctant to shake out their white pleats
JON despite the strength of this early May heat.
At the shady crossroads tall trees SPENCER
lean in to watch our tiny car arrive, BLUES
then all decide to pollinate at once.
EXPLOSION Every seed they have swims in the sky,
EXPLOSION so many flowers curling down
EXPLOSION toward the acacia snowglobe ground.
The breeze whips a yellow flood JON
in through the window SPENCER
across our knees BLUES and my cousin tells me
how wonderful the flowers are
battered, fried, then eaten whole.

The Lost

Nel mezzo del cammin di nostra vita
mi ritrovai per una selva oscura,
ché la diritta via era smarrita.

At one point, midway on our path in life
When I had journeyed half of our life's way
Half way along the road we have to go
    I came to in a gloomy wood
In the midway of this our mortal life
Midway upon the journey of our life
Midway along the journey of our life
    I came around and found myself now searching
    Through a dark wood, the right way blurred and lost

    I found me in a gloomy wood, astray
    I found I was in a dark forest
    I found myself within a forest dark
    I found myself within a shadowed forest
    I found myself obscured in a great forest
    Bewildered, and I knew I had lost the way

Halfway through the story of my life
    I woke to find myself in a dark wood
    Gone from the path direct
    For I had wandered off from the straight path
    For I had strayed from the straight path
    For I had lost the path that does not stray
    I'd wandered off the path, away from the light
Midway in our life's journey
    The straightforward pathway had been lost

Acknowledgements to various translations of Dante's *Inferno*, Canto I, lines 1-3, by Appelbaum, Cary, Carson, Kirkpatrick, Longfellow, Mandelbaum, Musa and Sisson, which have been remixed here.

Green Lake

(poem for a park in the Alps that floods once a year)

Diamond, a fish
tail that twists away
<   > me, bubble
formed in the mouth.
This flood of currents
once a year, a life, lifetime
once a minute, with you
or cut off from you. I wish
I had a diamond
which could stop time.
You know no one can say
how these fish arrived.
These flooded pathways
<   > everything
with light, a blanket,
invisible cloak for the eyes.
This is my lake. Will you
watch fish with me,
brush blades of weeds,
see bubbles swarm, more words
<   > with me?
The diamond is warmed
clear in our hands, familiar.
In this lake the world
ends, over and over.

Bliss

(after a talk about Douglas Dunn's archive at StAnza,
Scotland's International Poetry Festival)

This page in the poet's notebook starts
with a short story title I've forgotten.
Pause. Then comes the first poem
written after his wife's death.

A moment later we're shown another,
the first poem printed in his book *Elegies*:
'Re-reading Katherine Mansfield's
Bliss and Other Stories'.

It is almost funny, in the poem,
how the flattened fly punctuates
life in a book. This is the last
of the great paper archives.

The scholar carefully passes me
Dunn's copy of the source book
Bliss. I hold it. An old object.
Do I think it will be funny?

'Turn to the inside back,' he says,
'and tell me what you see.'
'The first draft of the poem,' I say.
He commands me. 'Read it.'

Starting slow, squinting in
at the black ink, biro I think,
handwritten loops, the bounce,
twirl, I read them, speeding up.

'This is crossed out. There
is a circle drawn round that...'
Rawness is struck through,
replaced by structure, calm.

Grief is formally rephrased
by a different time. I see
what I did not want to see
and choke on the final stanza.

'Thank you,' he says.
I pass the book along.
I cannot wait to run
out of the hall. Tears.

My face runs down the
street and I can only think
how much I want to tell you
this, how much I want

to tell you everything.

Sonnet for *Zookeeper*

Capture the set number of animals to complete the level[1]

crocodile drop lion delete crocodile
drop lion delete crocodile drop
lion delete crocodile drop lion
delete crocodile drop lion delete
monkey elephant delete swipe monkey
elephant delete swipe monkey elephant
delete swipe monkey elephant delete
swipe monkey elephant delete swipe
chain delete panda hippo chain
delete panda hippo chain delete
panda hippo chain delete panda
hippo chain delete panda hippo
giraffe swipe drop chain giraffe
swipe drop chain GAME OVER

[1] If you get tired, try pressing START to pause the game for a few seconds. Try looking away from the screen. Try staring at the ceiling and the shadows cast by the screen light. Imagine you are driving at night on a stretch of road lit by endless cat's eyes and have turned your headlights off.

It's not the despair, Laura…
it's the *hope*.

BRIAN STIMPSON, *Clockwork*

On Getting Boney M's Cover of 'Mary's Boy Child' by Harry Belafonte Stuck in My Head

I bump into a friend in the British Museum.
She tries to distract her son, Fin, with plaques
but he wants authentic plastic rainsticks,
white chocolate mummies, Peter Rabbit
in hieroglyphics, days of the week in Mayan honey.

Finlay has a poem:
        'I found a treasure.
        I measured the treasure.
        It was only a centimetre long.'

I shake the six-year-old's hand,
commenting on his chainmail vest,
gold crown and Jedi lightsaber.
I learn that he was born on a Tuesday
and admire his complete lack of pretension.

        He sings paper scarabs
        He sings Parthenon bookmarks
        He sings Centurion pyjamas
        He sings Harry Belafonte
        We sing rubber duck sphinxes
        We sing pencil elephants
        We sing İznik coffeecups
        We sing Rosetta Stone jigsaws

And how unaccountable the difference
between volume and worth. How fast
the heart can fill with treasure.

We make things new to make them new.
This is what we do.

Sheep
(for @dogsdoingthings)

Sheep wearing short pink diner uniforms, serving coffee,
    startling easily.
Sheep being followed through evening streets, sensing danger,
    flocking helplessly.
Sheep afraid in the nightclub chaos, hooves on the table,
    staring blankly.
Sheep in the jaws of persistent death, hearing
    come with me if you want to live.
Sheep on the run being told of the lamb that's yet to be born,
    the essential future.
Sheep hysterical, laughing, incredulous. Domestic sheep
    who can't balance a cheque book.
Sheep being taught to make household bombs, to fire guns,
    weave steel wool.
Sheep growing up on a motel bed. Sheep counting sheep,
    making love before dawn.
Sheep being found, corralled, being hounded. Sheep firing shots
    from a speeding car.
Sheep being blown from the tank's explosion, fighting metal
    with flesh, nearing exhaustion.
Sheep left nosing their lover's limp body. Sheep pulling
    themselves up. Sheep finishing it.
Sheep driving with a shotgun on the empty seat, their own dogs
    for protection, as the new life kicks.

from Groundhog Day

1

A polka on Gobbler's Knob
for Punxsutawney Phil
in a hatch, in a trunk of oak.
Prognosticator of Prognosticators,
can Spring be far behind?

7

A polka on Gobbler's Knob
for Punxsutawney Phil
in a hatch, in a trunk of oak.
Prognosticator of Prognosticators,
can Spring be far behind?

420

I need help. Dear Therapist,
drive this hog like ghosts
out of my seeing. Out –
I need a trumpet. Out –
I need release.

672

A polka on Gobbler's Knob
for Punxsutawney Phil
in a hatch, in a trunk of oak.
Prognosticator of Prognosticators,
can something be on my mind?

889

Dear Love, make a sound
like a chipmunk, so I may know thee.
Warm by the fire, we'll lie.

We all know winter is just
another step in the cycle.

1483

A polka on Gobbler's Knob
for Punxsutawney Phil
in the back of an armoured car,
in a pub, in a bar of oak.
Dipsomaniac of Dipsomaniacs,
can shots be far behind?

1569

Go ahead, babe. Make my day.
Dress like cowboys. Dress in snow.
Dress hot. Dress cold.
Dress at all, if you bother, if you dare.

2781

A polka. Gobbler's Knob.
A trunk of oak.
Spring is no longer able to attend.

3128

A polka on Gobbler's Knob.
Must stop this Punxsutawney Evil.
One paw on the wheel, looking angry.
The explosion can be seen for miles.

4270

Polka on Gobbler's Knob.
Toaster in the bath.

5271

Polka on Gobbler's Knob.
Shotgun in the mouth.

6943

Polka on Gobbler's Knob.
I've gone out the window.

7083

Polka. What?
Well then, I guess I'm a god.
I can tell you everything
and you will believe me.
But tomorrow...
Tomorrow.

9287

Finishing that book
in the diner
with a smile.

11784

Learning to play
the piano, to play
at learning, playing.

12301

Failing to save
the life of an old man.
To fail.

12395

Go and grab your
own trumpet now.
Let's polka.

The art of editing

can feel like working
for an origami factory
that's folded, a sculptor's
workshop that's gone bust,
for a transatlantic Zeppelin
maker who lost everything
in the '29 crash, but, really,
you are a diviner doing
well, a piano tuner who's
just grand, a plus-size
delicate but contemporary
ladies' glove manufacturer
who deserves a big hand.

Poem in Which I Respond to Notes Pencilled into the Margins of Ian Hamilton Finlay's *Selections*

Poems are toys and you're right: everyone plays with them in
their own way.

I did use my pram as a wheelbarrow once, wearing a red hood,
toys inside.

There's a note next to JOKES I'll ignore, though I like the line
below:

'What does not *die*; what matters – is that people should believe
in History.'

I would have noted ONLOOKER / SENDS FOR LEAF / BOAT

but echo WORDS ARE DIFFICULT / TO PUT INTO WORDS.

Take my shoes off
and throw them in the lake.

KATE BUSH, 'Hounds of Love'

Bedroom Filled With Foam

'If you want to watch something in bed, I will come and watch something in bed with you. If you want to go straight to sleep, I may stay up a little longer as I'm not ready to go to sleep just yet. If, for some reason, we can't get into the bedroom, say, because the bedroom is filled with foam, not that I'm saying I have filled the bedroom with foam or anything, but if it was filled with foam, we could always watch something down here.'

'Is it?'

'Is what?'

'Is the bedroom filled with foam?'

Wet Days Are the Worst

Wet days are the worst, when you find it impossible to shake me out of my most deeply rooted beliefs, when I sit in the bathroom banging my head against the door, repeating over and over: 'I believe the umbrella sellers are in league with the sky.'

Over Dave's Trousers

I knew you'd be out for ages, despite you saying you'd be home
early because you were starting early, so I planned to be out for
ages too only in a different part of town. I spilt some beer along
the length of the table and into Dave's trousers and even though
Dave was very nice about it, my guilt meant I remembered the
next thing he said to me with absolute clarity. He said:

'Everything is a test.'

Jam Trap

'My body is structurally going the way of gravity,' I said.

'Your brain will outlast your body, with luck,' you said.

'My brain?' I said. 'I think I have a brain like a jam trap.'

'What does that mean?' you said.

I shrugged, beaming like an idiot.

Where Have You Put the Wine?

'Where have you put the wine?'

'I've put the wine in the oven.'

'You've put the wine in the oven?'

'I haven't put the wine in the oven.'

'Where have you put the wine?'

'I've put the wine in the cold oven.'

'You've put the wine in the fridge?'

'I've put the wine in the fridge.'

Four Hours Away

I was telling you about visiting my cousins in Italy and how they took me up into the mountains north of Turin where I used to go as a girl and how far away it seems from everything and how my one cousin was telling me about bears that used to roam there while my other cousin was telling me about a trip they did up to one of the mountain lakes that took four hours to walk to and then I agreed with you when you said: 'I can't remember the last time I was four hours away from anything.'

Digital Ghost Towns

I forwarded you the thing about the British Library's web archiving project and you said it looked very interesting and I suddenly remembered that time I was trying to google some old poetry sites and kept seeing things like No Updates Since 1997 and how depressing it was and how somehow it was even more depressing seeing these digital ghost towns than it was for a physical magazine to simply stop making any new issues and then how the more I looked the more I realised the internet is full of dead ends and holes and the bits of it that actually work are just bright lights shining in a desert not like Vegas because Vegas is off-putting to lots of people so it's a bad analogy but I just mean that when the lights are working they're wonderful and anything abandoned especially something creative makes me sad but it's part of the process I suppose and we just have to try and avoid these holes and my god how many blogs will there even be online in 50 years' time and have we got another 2000 years of blogging coming up and shouldn't we be setting up grander projects that will last brightly forever without getting lost on the internet and just what are we playing at anyway?

'Shall we put the kettle on?' is what I actually say.

For here there is no place
that does not see you. You must change your life.

RILKE, 'Archaic Torso of Apollo'
(tr. Stephen Mitchell)

Reading Your Comics in Eype

I see Juggernaut's foot stamp down on San Francisco
as I read your latest in an armchair on the Dorset coast.
You'd nudged it towards my rucksack with a grin
when I was trying to pack my bedroll up at midnight
and now we're in the wind, in a weird chair, on an ancient cliff.
Juggernaut's foot glows with a purple light I don't understand
while on the beach below a fisherman sits tending his line.
I remember you saying how much you hate writing *Hope*,
the mutant who is meant to give hope to all the other mutants.
Now the fisherman's line is being bothered
by a mixed troupe of dogs along the rocks, and I wonder
if we get one, will you end up putting dogs in the X-Men,
imbuing them with special powers and names like *Howl*
and *Shake*, or is it just me who drags dogs into everything?
Superman had a dog once, who mourned his loss that time
when he went to space. He didn't want cats. He didn't want kids.
Oh, it's all so far away from these long waves and the wind,
so cold I'll have to go inside soon but I don't want to,
and I'm actually wearing a duvet, thinking *not yet, not yet*.
Please dogs, there's so much sea to write.
Today, I just want to listen to it.

The Burning of the Houses

Tottenham is on fire and I work in an arts centre
where the sky is blue and I can hear birdsong
from a sound installation of birds
cooing outside my office window.
This is London. Hackney is on fire now
and Jamie is looking up from his desk.
He stops working. He tweets that he can see
people smashing up a bus. He says there is a car
being soaked in petrol. He asks if there is someone
in that car. He tells us that car has been set alight.
This is London. Croydon is on fire now
and Anna is Facebooking furiously from Manchester
calling everyone bastards for doing this.
I am watching the BBC and reading Twitter
flicking between #LondonRiot and my friends.
Sometimes you can be proud of your friends.
I remember when Bianca came to stay
and we got tickets to watch *The Night
James Brown Saved Boston* in the QEH.
People are getting hurt. Television isn't going
to save us. But it's okay now, some of my friends
are linking to videos of kittens which must mean
everything is fine. This is London. It is on fire.
I go to bed while it is burning. I wake up
and parts of it are still burning.

Menagerie Speeches

1 *Zebra*

'I have just been to see Her Majesty
and I will form a majority menagerie.
I want to thank all those dear creatures
who screamed so hard for this success.
Zoo elections can be difficult
with so many lusting after pink hippogriffs,
lusting so profoundly after pink hippogriffs,
only to see their dreams turned into politics.
The menagerie I led did important screaming
and everything turns upon that vital hinge.
A good life is in reach for everyone willing
to scream their hardest for the proper thing.'

11 *Monkey*

'Thank you for your kindness, monkeys!
Monkeys, this is not the speech I wanted to give today
because I believe our Zoo needs a screaming menagerie!

I still do, but the beasts voted otherwise last night!
So I accept absolute and total bananas for our result
and pleasure myself to this, our Zoo insult.

I'm flinging out my resignation to the sky
but the argument of our campaign will not go away.
We will scream for screaming creatures once again!'

'I always expected this election to be difficult
given the complex concerns we've had to weigh.
Clearly those clowns' *poop* pranks have been more crushing
and unkind *poop poop* than anything I could say.

For that, of course, I must take responsibility
and therefore I announce I will resign.
poop poop A leadership election will now follow.
A new elephant, for a new time.'

Bird Talk

I would love to tickle your cat
but your cat has not been touched
for sixty years. If you are a woman,
I want to eat your cat. We all know
you're a stupid old cat. You probably
don't know what a real cat looks like.
Mention an eleven-year-old cat
and everyone loses their minds.
Come on – let's grab your cat right now!
How boring do we think your cat is?
I'll bet your cat reeks of turbot. I'll bet
you're just pretending to have a cat.
I wouldn't touch your cat if it was on fire.
I wouldn't eat your cat if it was made of gold.
I want to destroy your cat, annihilate it.
Karma is a cat, life a gargantuan female dog.

Post

Things have got so bad, you guys,
I'm rewatching *Prometheus*. Again.
And it feels like everything I'm feeling,
you know, it's such a piece of shit,
trying to be spiritual and failing,
wanting to be smart and flagging –
it makes my heart ache to see it.
Michael Fassbender is a robot
and everyone is getting drunk and
wearing unrealistic amounts of makeup.
Things happen for no good reason.
People in charge are needlessly cruel
and everyone is superstitious,
remembering the once-great glories
of their golden days, trying to appeal
to our once-great memories
and failing. Death permeates it.
Farce permeates it. And yet
it's so beautiful. Every person in it
is trying so hard to be great, doing
whatever they think is for the best, and
I'm hoping against tears that maybe
I just haven't understood, maybe
my anger isn't justified, and perhaps
this time I can get through the whole thing
without wanting to kill everyone.

We all go a little mad sometimes.

JOSEPH STEFANO, Norman Bates in *Psycho*

There Is an Epigraph

'Gather ye rosebuds while ye may'

> 'To the Virgins, to make much of Time', ROBERT HERRICK

'Every night I cut out my heart,
but in the morning it was full again.'

> Count Almásy, *The English Patient*, MICHAEL ONDAATJE

'I like my evil like I like my men – evil.'

> Buffy, *Buffy the Vampire Slayer* 4:9 'Pangs', JOSS WHEDON

'Realise that the grieving process will not take forever.
Time will eventually feel [sic] all wounds including this death.'

> 'How to Mourn the Death of a Dog', *eHow.com*, LUYOUNG

'I see dead people.'

> Cole Sear, *The Sixth Sense*, M. NIGHT SHYAMALAN

Moorhens

Give him a mask and he'll tell you the truth.

OSCAR WILDE

Red beak like a clay nose
you can put your face into,
tip dipped in yellow paint. On.
Ho, ho, ho. What have we here then?
The mask cannot be taken off again.

You've been eyed up by a devil,
tiptoeing round reeds in big steps.
Runners twitch. *Behind you.*
Scream with your legs in her face.
Scream with your long green legs.

She wants, she wants, she wants
you: blood slicked, in flux, fucked.
She will tear away your face
for a second's delight. *Ho, ho, ho.*
Punch's masked eyes glare red.

There are no dogs, no dripping jaws.
Sau-sa-ges? Just a reed trapdoor
making no demands beyond its own
existence. Police. The possibility of order.
Sau-sa-ges? Act like everything is fine.

Gently does it. Tiptoe on and gently
grows the lie. No one suspects a clown.
I say, I say, I say. Man in a bird mask,
black-feathered fool, bankside knave:
dig around the rushes for escape.

Here is confusion. Here is a demon
with dulled colours, long-clawed
and still calling you. *Ho, ho, ho.*
Who is willing to give up anything?
Who is willing to destroy anything?

But riverbanks know no sausages
and you will not suffer this derangement.
That's the way to do it. Breathe. *Scream.*
Stray feathers drift along the surface.
The water floods black with your joy.

Art Imitates Life, but Life Imitates TV
(after Ani DiFranco)

I watched *Lost* all last summer
because I wanted to be distracted.

I wanted plot holes that weren't my own
and I wanted polar bears.

I wanted to drown in the white sand sea
off a desolate island.

I wanted to watch people die,
in pain, in a horrible plane crash.

Murder, She Wrote

Angela – somebody told me there was a fire.
Are you hurt? Was anybody hurt? Angela –
Why is there blood on your hands – Angela?
Why is there blood on my hands? I've tried –
Angela – I've tried so hard to be good.

*

Angela – where is Jessica? Shouldn't she be here?
Her friends fall like leaves, the leaves, the leaves,
but she seems to hold on to her principles.
Angela – what do you mean 'There is no Jessica'?

*

I don't know what to do – Angela – what do you think?
Jessica wouldn't lie. I don't want to lie. But, okay –
Angela – let's take some time. Forget the murder,
or lack of one. I want to talk about you.
Do you think this is our blood?
Do you know I think about you all the time?

*

How did you make your way out of the story to find me?
Angela – not all plots are equal. You're amazing.
Please – Angela – please let me scream in whisper:
You're amazing. You're amazing. You're amazing.

*

A kiss from you – Angela – would be catastrophic.
Angela – an extinction level event – Angela –
like kissing the face of destruction. Do not tempt me –
Angela – we both understand the violence of a kiss.

*

Confusion is the proper state of love.
Angela – you draw the dagger out,
keep drawing, keep on drawing.
This dagger never ends.
It pierces the heart. It pierces the eye.
It pierces more lives than we are able to bear.
Let's hold hands in the cemetery – Angela –
where all the dead lie in their proper places.

*

O – may your face become a model of horror
to all who behold it. O – may blood slip from your eyes
as softly as silk. O – may your smile crack to twice
its beautiful width and may all your tears fall like skulls
into empty graves. Angela – I beg you. Stay.

*

You've never seen me crying, have you – Angela?
Come closer so you can taste the salt – Angela –
I will name each tear and let it run like a river
into the sea, the sea, the sea. I'll use the knife blade –
Angela – to carve tributaries from my eyes.
There is no evidence in support of love.
I will etch my face into a window of stained glass.
I will etch my face into a cathedral of disappointment.

*

There is to be no dramatic climax – Angela –
I wonder how your face would have looked,
frozen as the credits rolled over.
But there has been no death – Angela –
there's just us: two bungling murderers,
trying to avoid each other's eyes.

*

How often – Angela – does life give us
the opportunity to do the right thing? O –
Angela – O –

Every day –
Every day –
Every day.

Manifesto Based on Notes from Lars von Trier's
Five Obstructions

1

If you reveal yourself too soon
you make your own obstructions.

2

Don't show.
Tell the story.
Play with fragments,
crumbs you can find.

3

Minimise the distance
between the perfect
and the human.
With it, a bottle of Chablis.

4

Make something with no rules.
Make something that leaves a mark on you.
Listen to the perfect human living.
Write down 'tortoise'.

5

The room with no limits
is an empty room.
Experience something you hope to understand
in a few days.

Tigers

Tarmac. Broken lines are intersecting.
Fog lights on at 15 mph. Dark.
'Did you say you wanted 20?' The way
the shop assistant smelt as he leant in
to ask: a deep lustrous felinity.
(imaginary feathers warn the ground)
Dark. ONLINE BETTING ENTERS THE AGE
OF AQUARIUMS. Fog plumes are streaming down.
Line. Line. Line. Line. The cat's eyes keep time;
red eyes glowering on the left-hand side.
(better sorry than safe says the dead bird)
'William Hill are to take internet bets
on goldfish racing. They will take advice
from the most relevant goldfish experts.'
Headlights ignite the fog. *I tawt I taw...*
I think deceleration is the key.
Just keep moving.

Live life like you're gonna die.
Because you are.

WILLIAM SHATNER, 'You'll Have Time'

Tin Can Odyssey

*(for @Cmdr_Hadfield who posted his version of 'Space Oddity' online
the day before returning to Earth from the International Space Station)*

It's not just because it's good.
It's the *fact* of it. That view.
The fact that it exists as a view
and he exists to show it to us.
I woke up to it that morning,
stared at the Earth on fullscreen,
head still on my pillow, watching
the human music, lit continents,
all our revolutions from above.
I don't need a god looking down,
but the feeling that anyone could exist
in the black beyond the blue,
in the black behind the veil of daylight –
I found that view reassuring,
as if we finally, really, knew
it isn't just empty space.

Go

I

Louie Louie   *oh ho*
We gotta go

This is played by a brass band
marching over a body
in *The Naked Gun.*

When I go,
that's how
I want to go.

Louie Louie

II

When I go,
I want to go
on my back
listening to Chris, Isobel and Simon
talking about the white
extent of the sea,
the distant
stars.

III

Eaten by dogs.

IV

Daffodils,
heart
attack.

V

Struck by a trolley
listening to *Tristan and Isolde*
in Sainsbury's.

VI

I want to go in a pub
with gyoza and Asahi,
Giulia reminding me

everyone suffers

so you should only suffer
when you really have to.

VII

Telling David Bowie
he was wrong.

VIII

Juggled by killer whales.

IX

On the roof
of Royal Festival Hall,
looking over London,
wanting to hold your hand
as the sky ignites.

X

After you.

The Invisible Bear

- What goes up but never comes down?
- Your age.

We went into the dome in daylight.
Lights out for a fake night in darkness.
No hands and no faces. Nothing left at all
in fact, in plain sight, except for stars. Stars
spread out against the tile without cloud or dust.
So many stars, each one light years long away, unreachable.
So many stars, we could have tried, one day, to touch them.
So many stars, so many cold rocks and inert gases, so still.

Now accelerate. Lie back and think of being half-empty
or half-full. We fly into the stars right now so say goodbye
to the Earth over your shoulder, goodbye to your planet
in the rearview mirror. Goodbye horses, goodbye Boris Johnson,
goodbye the sun, the moon, all our wrong and stupid choices.

Here the world stops spinning. So take a look at this great bear.
Now we're flying into the bear. Now we're flying into and through
the bear, into and around and pivoting the whole of this great bear.
But this bear is invisible. This bear's joins cannot be seen.
There's no proof, and no legacy. All I can do is tell you
that your bear is here.

There's not much comfort in a bear you can see through, but then
in times of not much comfort, reach out for what you can. Now look,
spiral, back to the light, the sun, so small. Our planet, back with a fox,
is so small. This space, this now-bleak, now-black space between us
is all there is. This now-bleak, sun-black, half-full space between us
is all there is.

Go back, go back, go back. Plant your feet into the earth,
into the *Earth*. One step at a time is how we have to go.
Out of the dome, the doors are opened. You might say they have been
flung open without ceremony. But stop. Bear. Be dazzled by the daylight.

Stage Directions for *The Dog Always Wins*

Act I

[*Rome goes upstairs with a sword, quietly.*
It is still raining. Jules picks up her pen.
A loud knock startles her and she drops it.
The dog enters, grinning. Stage lights fade out.]

Act II

[*Love slowly raises his hammer. All die.*
He looks round, lonely. It is still raining.
Actions are heard whispering at the door.
The dog enters, grinning. Stage lights fade out.]

Act III

[*All the words move offstage and the rain stops.*
The soaked glamour pandas start to tap-dance.
At the back, a screen is slowly revealed.
The dog enters, grinning. Stage lights fade out.]

ACKNOWLEDGEMENTS

Thanks are due to the editors of the following publications and websites where some of these poems first appeared: *Adventures in Form* (Penned in the Margins, 2012), *Best British Poetry* (Salt Publishing, 2011), *Bird Book II* (Sidekick Books, 2012), *Cast: The Poetry Business Book of New Contemporary Poets* (Poetry Business, 2014), *Coin Opera 2: Fulminare's Revenge* (Sidekick Books, 2013), *Horizon Review, Lung Jazz: Young British Poets for Oxfam* (Cinnamon Press, 2012), *Magma, Modern Poetry in Translation, New Boots and Pantisocracies* (Smokestack Books, 2016), *Poems in Which, Poetry London, The Rialto, The Shuffle Anthology* (The Shuffle, 2011), *Silkworms Ink, Stop Sharpening Your Knives 5* (Egg Box Publishing, 2013), and *Test Centre*.

Some poems were also published in these pamphlets: *The Jam Trap* (Soaring Penguin, 2012), *Murder She Wrote* (p.o.w., 2012), *Flying into the Bear* (Happen*Stance* Press, 2013, shortlisted for the Michael Marks Awards), *ANGELA* (Sidekick Books, 2013), *Epigraphs* (if p then q, 2014, featured on BBC Radio 3's *The Verb*), and *Seven Poems* (Happen*Stance* Press, 2014).

'On Getting Boney M....', 'Sheep' and 'The Invisible Bear' were originally written for Roddy Lumsden's *BroadCast* reading series in London in 2011–12. 'Gone' was commissioned by Debbie Potts for the Cambridge University project *Modern Poets on Viking Poetry* in 2013.

Thank you also to my friends for their support, and in particular to Helena Nelson for her encouragement and comments in the early drafting of this manuscript; Neil Astley for publishing it and sending me photos of himself dressed as a bear; A.B. Jackson, Kathryn Maris and Simon Barraclough for invaluable feedback; Richard Scott, Ed Doegar, Anna Selby, John Canfield and Joey Connolly for being delightful; and Kieron, who is always there, under everything.